Jacki Wadeson's Beautiful
Braids, Bea
and Bows

southwater

This edition is published by Southwater

Distributed in the UK by
The Manning Partnership
251–253 London Road East
Batheaston, Bath BA1 7RL
tel. 01225 852 727 fax 01225 852 852

Published in the USA by
Anness Publishing Inc.
27 West 20th Street, Suite 504
New York, NY 10011
fax 212 807 6813

Distributed in Canada by
General Publishing
895 Don Mills Road
400–402 Park Centre
Toronto, Ontario M3C 1W3
tel. 416 445 3333 fax 416 445 5991

Distributed in Australia by
Sandstone Publishing
Unit 1, 360 Norton Street
Leichhardt
New South Wales 2040
tel. 02 9560 7888 fax 02 9560 7488

Southwater is an imprint of Anness Publishing Limited
Hermes House, 88–89 Blackfriars Road, London SE1 8HA
tel. 020 7401 2077; fax 020 7633 9499

© Anness Publishing Limited 1996, 2001

Publisher: Joanna Lorenz
Senior Editor: Caroline Beattie
Photographer: John Freeman
Hair Stylist: Debbi Finlow
Designers: Tony Sambrook, Edward Kinsey

Previously published as *Creative Fun: Braiding Fun*

1 3 5 7 9 10 8 6 4 2

Introduction

Doing your hair is so much fun, and you'll be surprised to see how easy it is to create different styles. There are lots of things you can do, whether your hair is straight, wavy, or curly. All you need is a brush and comb, and as many brightly colored ribbons, beads, bows, ponytail holders, and flowers as you can find. Ask your mother if you can raid her sewing box: you'll find lots of interesting things you can use. Practice making a simple braid and ponytail first, as these form the basis of many styles. It's great if you have a friend to help, so you can do each other's hair. Mix and match ribbon colors to go with your favorite clothes. You can jazz up a plain T-shirt or give an outfit a whole new look just by changing your hair.

Happy braiding!

Jacki Wadeson

Contents

GETTING STARTED

BRAIDING FUN

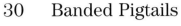
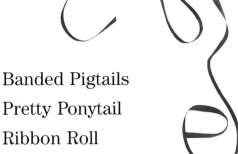

Simple Braid

A three-stranded braid is a lot easier than it looks.

1 Part your hair in the middle, from the front to the nape of your neck. Divide one half into three equal sections and hold the outer sections of hair with your hands.

2 Cross the right section over the center section. Use your fingers to make sure that the other two sections remain separate.

3 Now cross the left section over the new center section. It is important to pull all three strands of hair evenly as you work, so that your braid is straight.

4 Now you can see how the braid is beginning to form. Carry on braiding, crossing the sections, right over center and left over center.

5 Hold the end of your braid about 2 in from the end. Take a ponytail holder and slip it over the end, then twist it back over as many times as you need to keep the braid secure.

Perfect Ponytail

A ponytail is one of the easiest styles to do. It keeps hair tidy and stops it getting into a tangle.

1 Brush your hair straight back, using long sweeping strokes to make sure there are no knots. Tease any knots out by brushing gently from the bottom.

2 Place a scrunchie on your wrist, then pull your hair together with your hands at the back of your head.

4 Thread the ponytail through the scrunchie again (your hands will swap positions) and repeat.

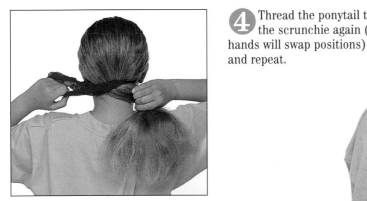

3 Slip the scrunchie off your wrist and over the ponytail. Hold your hair in one hand and twist the scrunchie with the other.

7

Twist & Roll

A really simple style that can be done in a jiffy, using a long fabric-covered band and a few twists of your wrists.

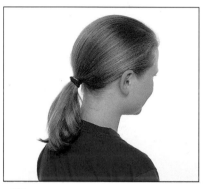

1 Brush your hair into a ponytail at the nape of your neck (see page 7). Secure with a ponytail holder.

2 Take a long fabric-covered band and place it under your ponytail. Cross over the ends over the top and hold them in your hands.

3 Twist the fabric band around the ponytail, right down the length of your ponytail, until you reach the end.

4 Tuck covered hair up and under, then cross the ends of the fabric band over one another to secure them.

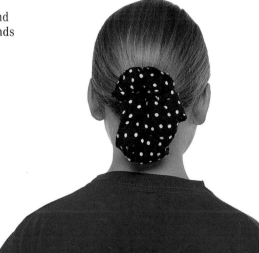

8

Do the Flip

A nifty way to wear your ponytail – you just need a Topsy Tail to flip it up and thread it down.

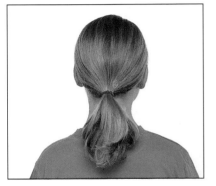

1 Brush your hair straight back and secure at the nape of your neck with a ponytail holder.

2 Gently push the straight end of the Topsy Tail down the back of your head, between your neck and the ponytail holder.

3 Hold the straight end of the Topsy Tail and thread your ponytail through the loop. Pull the Topsy Tail down and your hair will flip through.

9

Beading

Add colorful beads – as many as you like – to brighten up your hair.

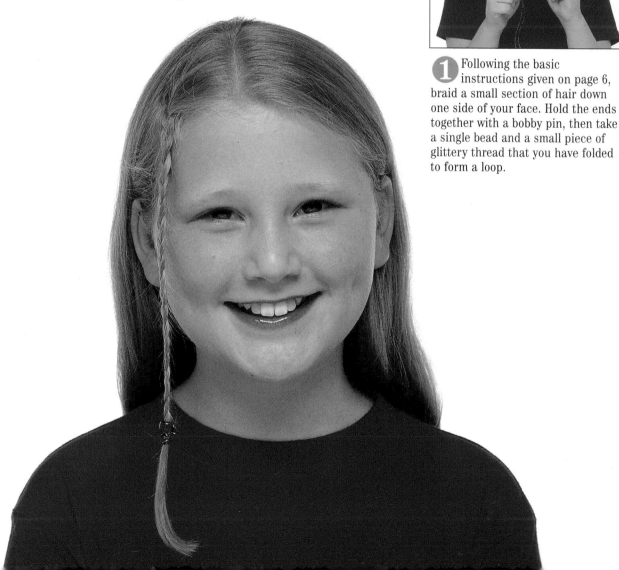

1 Following the basic instructions given on page 6, braid a small section of hair down one side of your face. Hold the ends together with a bobby pin, then take a single bead and a small piece of glittery thread that you have folded to form a loop.

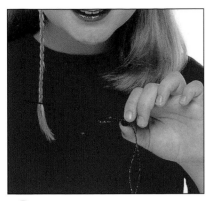

2 Pass the looped end of the thread through the center of the bead. This is easier if you make sure that the beads you use have quite large holes in the middle.

3 Remove the bobby pin from the end of the braid and pass the braid through the loop of thread. Make sure you keep a firm hold on the bead, so it doesn't fall off.

4 Push the bead toward the braid, then pull the ends of the thread; your braid will start pulling through the center of the bead. Continue pulling until the end of the braid comes through the bead.

5 Wrap the thread around and around the end of your braid, making sure the strands lie flat, until you have covered about $\frac{1}{2}$ in of hair below the bead.

6 Tie the ends of the thread, then repeat to form a knot. If necessary, cut the ends of the thread off, being careful not to snip the end of your braid.

TIP

Make sure you always keep your beads in a safe place away from babies or small children, who may think they are candy.

Accessories

Barrettes, headbands and floppy
bows change your look in an instant.

2 Smooth your hair back and
secure it with a zigzag
headband that fastens at the back of
your neck, underneath your hair.

3 Take the front section of your
hair and clasp it in a ponytail
holder that has been decorated with
short pieces of ribbon.

1 Scoop your hair up into a ponytail on top of your head and
secure it with a ponytail holder.

4 Scoop the front hair back from the ears to the crown and clip on a chiffon bow.

5 Add a neat velvet scrunchie to dress up a low ponytail.

6 Secure the front hair back with a large tortoiseshell barrette.

9 Thin ribbon bows make tiny braids look extra special.

7 Headbands come in all shapes and sizes and simply slide into place.

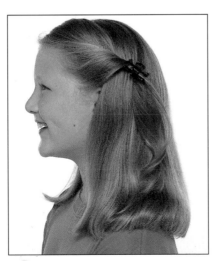

8 Take a small section of hair, twist it up and over and secure it with a mini clip.

13

Perfect Pigtails

Any length of hair can be scooped up into pretty pigtails. Add bright ribbons in fun colors for a daytime look and fairy bows for party time.

TIP
Gift-wrapping ribbon is ideal for making bows and covering bobby pins.

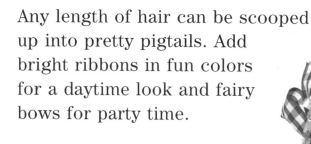

1 Part your hair in the middle from front to back. Put a ponytail holder on one hand, so that it sits on your knuckles (this makes it easy to slip over your bunch) and hold one half of your hair in the other hand.

2 Slip the hair all the way through the holder, gripping your hair tightly with one hand and using your thumb to pull the band tight.

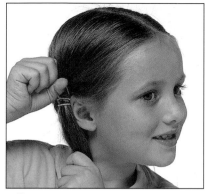

3 Twist the ponytail holder around once, then put your fingers through the loop and pull the bunch through. Do this again until it is tight enough to hold your hair.

4 Take a short piece of ribbon and tie it around the pigtail, then make a bow. Repeat for the other side.

5 For fairy bows, twist thin ribbon, around the top half of a barrette, starting at the open end. Tie a tiny bow at the end of each barrette. Use lots of different colors, and simply push the bobby pins into place around your hairline.

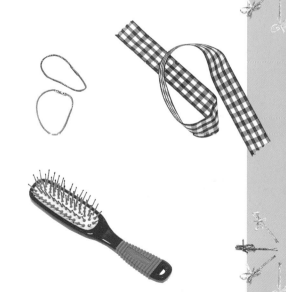

Heidi Hi

1 Part your hair in the middle from front to back. Comb half over one shoulder and divide into three equal sections. Then braid right down to the ends of the hair.

2 Take a terrycloth ponytail holder and push it over one hand so that it sits on your knuckles. Hold the end of the braid in the other hand. Don't let go or it will unravel.

3 Comb the other half of your hair over to the front of your shoulder and braid in the same way. Try to keep your braids even by pulling equally on each section of hair.

4 Secure the end of the braid in a terrycloth holder, as before, making sure it is tight enough to hold your braid.

5 You can either leave your braids down or pin them on top of your head with a novelty barrette.

16

Once you have learned how to braid your hair, you can start experimenting with different types of holders and looping the braids over your head.

TIP

Use a comb to practice getting your part straight. Your hairstyle will look even better if your part doesn't wriggle around like a snake!

17

Topsy Turvy

A topknot is great if you are growing out your bangs, because you can tuck in all those little ends that tend to stick out.

TIP

You can twist ribbons together for a really unusual headband. Choose colors that match your clothes.

1 Brush your hair through to make sure you haven't got any tangles. Use the thumb of each hand to divide off the top section of the hair from your ears up to the top of your head.

2 Push a scrunchie over the fingers of one hand so that it rests on your knuckles, and clasp the topknot of hair in your other hand.

3 Slip the scrunchie over the hair and twist it, ready to repeat. Be careful not to let go of the topknot while you are twisting the scrunchie around it.

4 Twist the scrunchie around again in exactly the same way. If it seems a little loose, twist again until the topknot feels nice and firm. The number of times you need to twist depends on how big your scrunchie is.

5 You can dress up your topknot by taking two differently colored thin ribbons and placing them around your head like a headband. Simply tie the ends at the back of your neck, under your hair, where no one can see.

19

French Fancy

Straight chin-length hair looks great with small braids when they are cleverly twisted to give a trendy teen style. An unusual barrette (we found a beautiful pair of elephants) adds the perfect finish.

1 Part off a small section of hair on the top of your head. Lift the front of this section and start braiding. As you cross the strands, bring a little more hair into the outer strands and work into the braid.

TIP
You can decorate plain barrettes by sticking pictures or buttons on them.

2 Take a small section of hair at the side of your head, in front of your ear, and braid from the roots to the ends. When you reach the ends, secure with a ponytail holder.

3 Take another small section of hair at the other side of your head in front of your ear and braid in the same way, until you reach the ends. Secure with another holder.

4 Take the two side braids and bring them to the top of your head. Secure these and the end of your top braid in a large barrette that will cover all the ends.

5 For a quick change, tie the ends of the braids in a scrunchie and divide the back hair into two neat little pigtails with matching scrunchies.

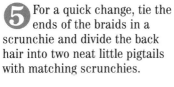

Beaded Braids

1 Part your hair in the center, then take a small section of hair and divide into three equal strands. Begin to braid, working down from the roots to the ends. See page 6 for full directions.

2 Slip the beads over the end of the braid, as shown on pages 10–11. Attach a second bead in the same way and bind the ends with thread so the beads don't fall off.

3 Make as many more braids as you would like; we did three on each side. Make sure that you put the beads on at the same level on all the braids.

4 Brush the loose hair up high on the crown of your head and secure with a scrunchie. Brush the ponytail through so it's nice and smooth.

Tiny braids with beads threaded through the ends look difficult to do but are so easy. Bead just a few braids around your face or ask a friend to help you do them all over your head.

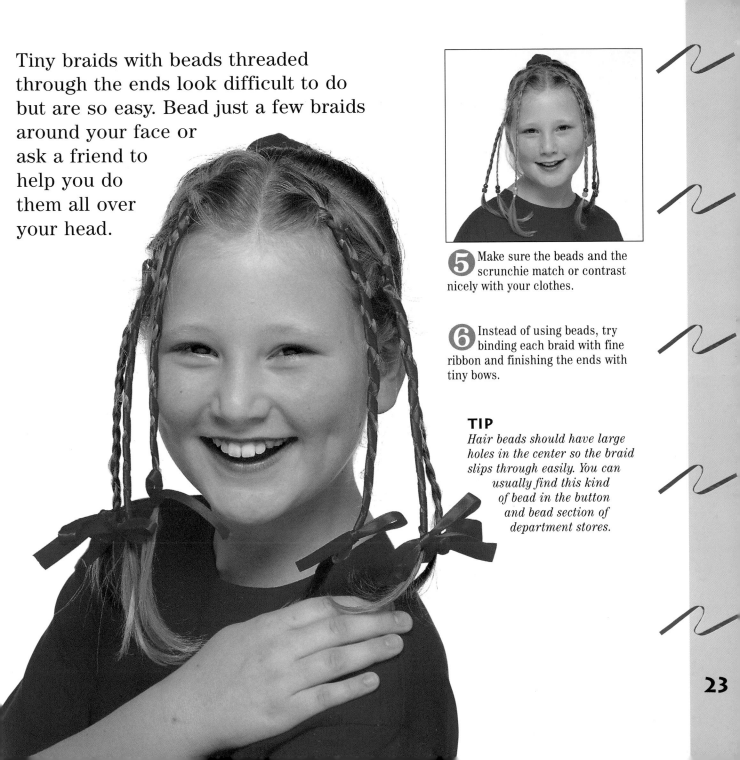

5 Make sure the beads and the scrunchie match or contrast nicely with your clothes.

6 Instead of using beads, try binding each braid with fine ribbon and finishing the ends with tiny bows.

TIP
Hair beads should have large holes in the center so the braid slips through easily. You can usually find this kind of bead in the button and bead section of department stores.

Tiny Twists

Finely braided hair need not look the same every day. It can be twisted into tiny coils and brightened up with multicolored ponytail holders.

TIP

Fine braids like these can be left in for weeks, but it is best to remove hair accessories at night so they don't pull your hair or get tangled up.

24

1 Take about six thin braids in one hand and twist them together. You will find that the hair starts to roll back on itself and begins to form a coil.

2 Continue twisting, allowing the hair to coil around the finger of your other hand, then carefully tuck the ends of the braids in, so the hair feels secure.

3 Push a small ponytail holder over the first two fingers of one hand and use the other hand to hold the coil of hair. Carefully slip the band over your hair and push it down so the braids are held tight.

4 Make as many more twists as you want. We did four at the front and one in the center at the back. If you would like more, simply use fewer braids for each twist.

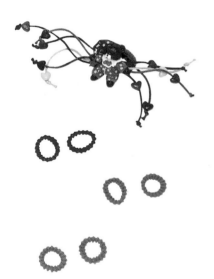

Racy Ribbons

Braids look really good if you include ribbons as you go. At the ends tie each ribbon into a bow for a really beautiful cascade of color.

TIP
Cut ends of ribbons on a slant to stop them fraying.

1 Part your hair in the center and brush it through. Gather up the hair at each side and use ponytail holders to secure in pigtails. Make the pigtails at about ear level.

2 Take three ribbons, each of a different color. Pull the ends halfway through the holder, then tie them onto it once. Make sure the ends are roughly even.

3 Divide the hair into three sections and put two matching pieces of ribbon with each one. Now begin braiding as normal right down to the ends.

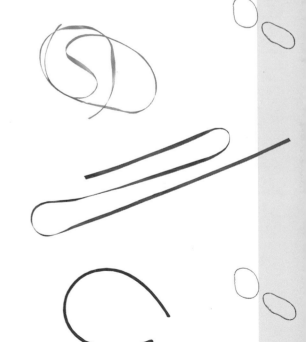

4 Secure the end of the braid, with the ribbons, in a ponytail holder. Now take each pair of matching ribbons and tie them in a bow. Repeat with the other side.

5 You could always pop on a matching headband or add a bow at the top of each braid.

Braids & Bows

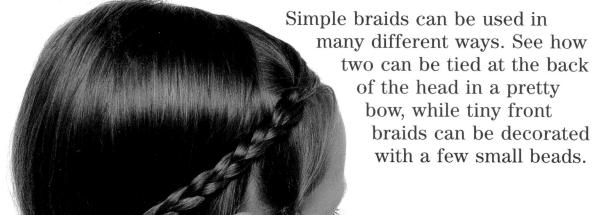

Simple braids can be used in many different ways. See how two can be tied at the back of the head in a pretty bow, while tiny front braids can be decorated with a few small beads.

TIP

You could make a multicolored beaded holder yourself. Thread beads onto lots of tiny lengths of cord and then tie them around a ponytail holder.

1 Part your hair in the center then take a small section of hair from one side. Start braiding near the roots and work all the way down to the ends. See page 6 for full details on how to braid.

2 Take a small section of hair from the other side of your head and braid in exactly the same way. Secure the ends of each braid in a ponytail holder, twisting the holder until it holds tight.

3 Pull the braids to the back of your head. Tie them together with a ribbon and make a bow.

4 Braid two more sections of hair, so that each one hangs in front of your ear. Thread three differently colored beads onto each braid. (See pages 10–11 for details.) It looks nice if at least one of the beads matches your ribbon.

5 Finally, brush your hair (taking care not to spoil the braid or the bow) for a sleek finished look.

Banded Pigtails

Keep your pigtails neat by wrapping bands of color around them all the way to the bottom.

TIP

Design your own bands by sewing novelty buttons onto terrycloth ponytail holders.

1 Part your hair in the middle from front to back. Put a ponytail holder over one hand so it sits on your knuckles, then slip it over one section of hair. Twist it back over until it's tight. Repeat for the other pigtail.

2 Take two terrycloth holders (we used ones with little piggies on) and slip one over each bunch. You may need to twist them twice so they hold nicely.

3 Take two more differently colored terrycloth holders and slip a pigtail through each band, about 2 in from the first band.

4 Take more colored holders and continue adding them to your pigtails, always about 2 in from the last, until you run out of hair – or bands!

5 Make sure the holders are at the same levels all the way down both pigtails. Why not clip pretty barrettes above each pigtail?

Pretty Ponytail

1 Tip your head and brush your hair forward from the back of your neck right to the ends. Make sure there are no tangles or knots. It is easier if you use a brush with wide spaces between the bristles.

2 Hold your hair with one hand and run the fingers of your other hand through your hair to make sure it is smooth. Keep hold of your hair and lift your head up.

3 Put a scrunchie over the knuckles of one hand, then pull your hair though it. Twist the scrunchie and pull your hair through again until it is tight enough.

5 Use differently colored scrunchies, as it looks good if the colors cross over and form a pattern. Pin little net flowers in place with bobby pins to add an extra splash of color.

4 Add two more scrunchies above the first one so that you get lots of height.

32

A really high ponytail, right on the top of your head, makes you instantly taller and is one of the easier styles to do.

TIP
You can get fabric flowers in the sewing sections of department stores. Push a bobby pin into the back of each flower to help you to fasten them into your hair.

Ribbon Roll

1 Use a comb with widely spaced teeth to help you smooth your hair up to the top of your head. Hold your hair with one hand and put a ponytail holder over the other hand. Twist the holder around your hair to make a ponytail.

It's easy to make very curly hair look neat and tidy if you braid a high ponytail with ribbon and twirl it into a roll.

2 Braid the ponytail from the top down to the ends and secure the ends with another ponytail holder. You could leave your hair just like this if you wanted to.

3 Take a ribbon and slip one end under the ponytail holder at the top of your head and pull through, so the ends are even. Bind the ponytail with the ribbon right down to the ends.

4 Take the end of the braid, with the ribbon ends, in one hand and roll it around on itself to make a bun. Use one or two barrettes to secure it in place but allow the ends of the ribbon to fall free.

5 We added a dark blue, pale blue, and white cord headband to change the look into one ideal for parties. A headband is useful for keeping your hair off your face.

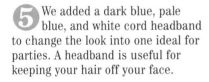

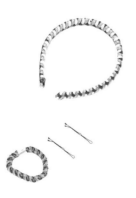

Triple Twist

1 Brush your hair into a low ponytail at the nape of your neck. Make sure the front is really smooth with no ends sticking out.

This is a perfect style if your hair is thick and wavy. The hair is divided into three and braided, then the three braids are formed into one. It looks complicated but is so easy to do.

TIP

Look in your mom's sewing box for scraps of fabric and ask her to help you make your own fabric bands.

2 Divide the ponytail into three equal sections. Take the first one and braid it from top to bottom. Look again at the instructions on page 6 if you need help braiding.

3 When you get to the end of the braid, secure it with a ponytail holder. Braid the other two sections in exactly the same way. You now have three braids to work with.

4 Take the three single braids and braid them together in the same way as before. Your hair will form into a thick braid that looks like a twist of hair.

5 Simply twist another ponytail holder to hold the hair in one place. Or add two multicolored chiffon hair accessories to the end of the twist for a different look.

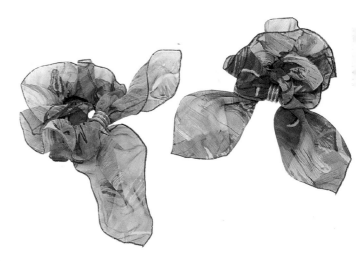

37

Pony Princess

Here the top section of your hair is smoothed back and the rest of the hair held by cute yarn-covered bands to give a multicolored ponytail.

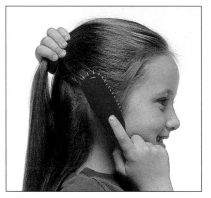

1 Brush your hair so there are no tangles or knots. Then use your thumbs to divide off the top section of your hair. Hold this section tightly with one hand.

2 Use a yarn-covered band to secure this top section of hair. You may need to twist once or twice so the band is tight enough to hold the hair properly.

3 Gather all your hair together at the nape of your neck and secure it in another yarn-covered band of a different color. You may need to twist it again so it's tight enough to stay in place.

TIP
Covered bands like these are made from flexible wire sewn into the edge of a long strip of fabric.

4 Take another colored band and do the same thing again. The bands should sit neatly next to one another, so push them together.

5 Add another colored band further down the ponytail. Or take a bendy fabric band, place it around the back of your head and bring the ends up on top in the front. Twist the ends into a circle to hold the band in place.

Be-Bop Pigtails

High bunches like these are really easy to do on chin-length hair, and you can twist a section with ribbon for a really grown-up look, too.

1 Part your hair in the center and brush your hair so it is really smooth. Take a small section at one side and brush again. You can experiment to see how large a section you'd like to use.

TIP

To make your hair shiny, always use cool water for the final rinse after you shampoo your hair.

2 Tie this small piece of hair in a ponytail holder. We used silky crocheted holders in multicolors, which look really good.

3 Twist the band until it is tight enough to hold the hair in place. Repeat for the other side.

4 Divide off a small section of the hair from one of the bunches and slip the end of a ribbon halfway through the covered band. Twist the ribbon around your hair and tie the ends in a bow.

5 For that extra-special look, push bobby pins through tiny fabric flowers of matching colors and use them as pretty accessories near one of the pigtails.

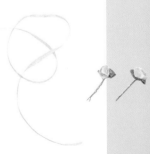

41

Bobbie Braids

1 Divide the top section of your hair into two sets of braids. Take one section in one hand and slip a ponytail holder over the other hand. You can use a plain holder or one with beads attached to it.

2 Slip the holder over the braids, twist round and slip the braids through the ponytail holder again until it is tight enough to hold. Try to position the beads so they are at the front.

3 Take another holder and tie it around the ends of the braids, twisting around until it is tight enough to hold. Again, position the beads so they are at the front. Repeat with the other side.

4 Take all the back braids in one hand and slip over another ponytail holder close to the back of your head to make a ponytail.

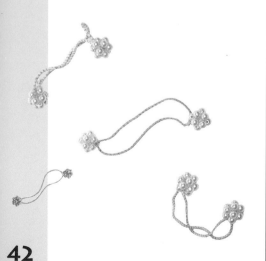

TIP
You can make beaded holders like the ones we used by threading about eight beads onto thin elastic and tying it onto plain holders.

42

Braiding hair all over the head is a traditional and practical way to keep it neat and tidy. Adding pretty accessories can give you a new look each day.

5 Tie the end of the ponytail in a matching holder to form a little tail.

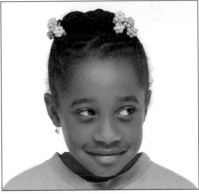

6 Twist both side ponytails into each other over the top of your head.

Mini Ha Ha

1 Part the hair in the center and split off a section on one side. Braid as described on page 6 and then secure the ends in a covered band.

Mid-length hair can be triple-braided and then bound at the ends with multicolored holders.

TIP

If you have flyaway hair ask your mother if you can borrow a silk scarf. Use the scarf to cover a bristle brush and stroke it over your hair. The static electricity, which makes hair wispy, magically disappears.

2 Make five more braids in exactly the same way. There should be one either side at the front, two behind your ears, and two at the back.

3 Gather three braids together at one side and then plait these from roots to ends. The plait will be bulky to work with but is still easy to do. Secure with a ponytail holder.

4 Repeat for the other side, working exactly as before. Secure with a ponytail holder, covering the other holders to make it look as if the braids have been bound.

5 You can also add a headband and bind the braids with fine matching or contrasting ribbon, finishing off with a bow.

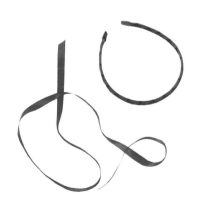

Clever Cornrows

Cornrow braids look brilliant in pigtails and are ideal for beading and adding bows.

TIP:
When washing cornrow-braided hair, rinse it thoroughly after shampooing to remove all the suds. This prevents the scalp getting dry and feeling itchy and uncomfortable.

1 Braid tiny sections of hair working close to the head. You will need the help of your mother or a friend to do the back and sides. Be patient as it will take some time.

2 Divide all the front braids into two equal bundles. Take one bundle in your hand and secure in a ponytail holder, then repeat for the other side.

3 Gather up all the braids at the back into one hand. Take a ponytail holder and slip it over, twist the band, and repeat until it is tight enough to hold the ponytail.

4 You can add two beads to each braid, or just to some. If you want instructions on how to do this, see pages 10–11. You could use lots of different beads on each braid or choose them to match your clothes.

5 You can also add tiny bows to the tops and bottoms of the pigtailed braids. Use lots of thin, colorful ribbons for this.

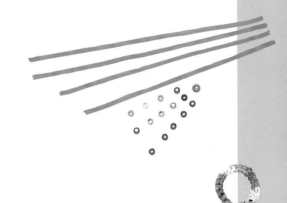

47

Top & Tail

A simple braid takes on a party look if it is topped and tailed with scrunchies.

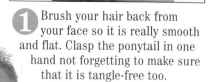

1 Brush your hair back from your face so it is really smooth and flat. Clasp the ponytail in one hand not forgetting to make sure that it is tangle-free too.

TIP
If you find you have lots of little pieces of hair sticking out, simply wet your hands and smooth over your hair to lay them flat.

② Take a scrunchie and push it over one hand so it rests on your knuckles. Pass the ponytail through the scrunchie, twisting until it is secure enough to hold your hair firmly.

③ Divide the ponytail into three equal sections and braid it from top to bottom. Work right down until you are 2 in from the bottom.

④ Take a matching scrunchie and use it to secure the end of the braid. You may have to twist it up to three times to make sure it is tight enough.

⑤ The result is a decorative and neat braid. For a more grown-up look, twist the braid around into a bun, and secure it with a ponytail holder. Add three bobby pins decorated with rosebuds to match.

49

Tufty Topknot

This fun style is really easy to do and is ideal for cornrow-braided hair.

1 Scoop all the front braids together and hold them in place with one hand. Take a ponytail holder in the other hand then slip it onto the braids. Twist to secure.

2 Divide the bunch of braids into three equal sections and braid each set together to form a tuft of braids. Twist the ends together.

3 Gather all the back braids together and secure them with a ponytail holder. Try to do this in the center of the back of your head so it looks neat.

TIP

If you have a plain bow you can make it extra special by sewing on some unusual beads or buttons. Ask your mother if you can look in her sewing box for something suitable.

4 Clip a large, floppy bow to the topknot. You can secure it through the ponytail holder if you like. Make sure the bow is right in the center.

5 For a party look, tie a short ribbon into a bow round the topknot and at the end of each tuft. Curl tiny lengths of paper ribbon (scrape your thumbnail along each one) then attach to bobby pins and fasten them in your hair.

Wonder Waves

Straight hair can be changed into a mass of waves by using soft curlers, but you do need to leave them in overnight to get the best result.

1 Take a soft curler and fold it in half to grip a section of hair between the two pieces. Pull the curler right down to the bottom of the hair.

52

2 Wind the soft curler up the hair from the ends toward your head. Do this slowly and make sure you don't let go of either end of the curler.

3 When you can wind no further, take the ends of the soft curler and bring them both together, then cross them over. This is so that they hold the hair in place.

4 Repeat all over your head. Remember, the bigger the sections of hair you wind, the looser the wave will be. For really tight curls, take only small sections and use lots of curlers.

TIP

You will get an even curlier effect if your hair is just very slightly damp. But remember never to go to bed with wet hair.

5 Leave your curlers in overnight. They are very soft so they won't keep you awake!

6 In the morning remove each curler and use your fingers to "rake" through each wave. You could also scoop the front hair back and secure it with a sunflower barrette.

53

Teeny Bopper

1 Lift a section of hair from the front to the top of your head and then use a bristle brush to smooth the front of your hair. Do not brush through the length of your hair or you will pull the waves out.

2 Take a large ponytail holder (one that will wrap round lots of times) and use it to secure the top hair. Make sure you do this right in the middle, because you don't want your topknot to be lopsided.

3 Take a section of hair at one side and fasten it with another large holder in a different color. Loosen the waves with your fingers, but don't brush or comb the length of your hair.

4 Do exactly the same on the other side using another ponytail holder in a different color. You can, if you wish, secure more bands like this at the crown.

Once you have waved your hair, you can create lots of other looks. Here, a trio of holders tames the waves and gives a fresh new style.

TIP

If you want to keep your waves for as long as possible, only rake through them with your fingers or use a wide-toothed comb.

Braided & **B**ound

Long, straight hair can be braided, then wrapped with different colored ribbons for a really snazzy style.

1 Take small sections of hair and braid them tightly from roots to ends. See page 6 for full instructions on how to braid. You may need a friend to help you to braid the hair at the back.

2 Secure the end of each braid by wrapping with fine colorful thread. Wrap it round a couple of times before tying into a tight knot. Snip off any long ends, but be careful not to cut your hair.

3 Take a piece of narrow ribbon and fold it in half. Tie the ribbon to the top of the braid, then bind downward by crossing the ribbon over and over, first at the front of the braid, then at the back.

4 Continue binding until you reach the end of the braid and tie the ends of the ribbon. Repeat until you have bound all your braids. You may need a helping hand to do the braids at the back.

5 Scoop up the braids on the top of your head and bind them into a topknot with narrow ribbon.

TIP
Thin ribbons can be left in your hair overnight because they are soft and won't pull your hair.

Crimping Crazy

1 Divide your hair into thin sections and braid it from the roots to the ends making the braids even and quite tight. The smaller the sections are, the finer the finished crimp will be.

2 Secure the end of each braid with a piece of thread, wrap it around two or three times, and then tie the ends into a little knot. If you prefer, you can use very small ponytail holders.

3 Leave the braids overnight to set your hair into its new shape. You can lightly mist your hair with water if you wish but don't go to bed with wet hair.

4 In the morning carefully unravel each braid, loosening it with your fingers as you go.

TIP
Crimps will stay in your hair until you next wash it.

58

Older girls use crimping irons to create ripples in their hair, but you can get the same effect by braiding your hair and leaving it overnight to set.

5 You can, if you wish, gently comb through using a wide-toothed comb or a brush with widely spaced teeth.

6 Keep your hair away from your face with a multicolored headband.

Double Dazzle

Once you have crimped your hair you can create different styles with it.

1 Gently brush through your hair, but don't tug or pull too much or you will loosen the crimps. Divide off a section of your hair at the front and hold it tightly in one hand.

TIP

Paper flowers that are used to decorate presents make perfect hair accessories. You can find them in stationery shops or large department stores.

2 Take a ponytail holder and place it over the knuckles of the other hand. This makes it easier to secure the hair. Do not let go and hold the section tight to your head.

3 Pull your hair through the holder, then twist the holder and pull the hair through it again. Repeat until it is tight enough to hold the hair in place. Push the band close to your head.

4 Repeat for the other side, making another pigtail in exactly the same way. Try to make sure you use about the same amount of hair in each pigtail.

5 Smooth the pigtails down with your hands or a soft brush, but don't brush too hard! You could also take another section of hair on your crown and bunch it with a holder.

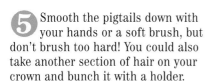

61

Braided Flips

Braids can be bound tightly with cord for a really unusual style.

1 Part your hair in the center, then braid the hair on one side from the roots to the ends. Keep the tension even so that your braid is straight.

TIP

To bind braids, choose cord that is not too shiny, so that it doesn't slip off the braid.

2 Secure the end of the braid with a ponytail holder, twisting it back until it is tight enough to hold. Repeat on the other side, making a braid in the same way.

3 Take a piece of fine cord and, starting at the top, bind the braid by wrapping the cord around and around it. Keep the spirals of cord close to one another.

4 Halfway down your braid, you can change the color of the cord. Hold the ends of the old and new colors against the braid and bind the color tightly around the ends. Continue working right down to the end of your braid, and secure the end of the cord by tucking it into the ponytail holder.

5 Add two flowers or matching barrettes to either side of your head, at the front or above the braids.

ACKNOWLEDGMENTS

The Publishers would like to thank the following girls for modeling for this book:
Lauren Andrews, Charley Crittenden, Kimberley Durrance, Terri Ferguson, Sophia Groome, Nicola Kreinczes, Elouisa Markham, Tania Murphy, Lucy Oliver, Kim Peterson, Alexandra Richards, Leigh Richards, Kate Yudt.

The Publishers would also like to thank the following for lending hair accessories, brushes, combs, and other equipment:
Boots; Head Gardener, Knightsbridge; Lady Jayne; Mason Pearson, Kent; Molton Brown; Tesco.

This book is designed for children between the ages of 8 and 12. All beads, bows, threads, and hair accessories should be kept out of reach of babies and small children.